Let Freedom Ring

The Declaration of Independence

By Lora Polack Oberle

Consultant:
David W. Young
Education Director
Atwater Kent Museum of Philadelphia History
Philadelphia, Pennsylvania

Bridgestone Books
an imprint of Capstone Press
Mankato, Minnesota

Bridgestone Books are published by Capstone Press
151 Good Counsel Drive • P.O. Box 669 • Mankato, Minnesota 56002
http://www.capstone-press.com

Printed in the United States of America

Library of Congress Cataloging-in-Publication Data
Oberle, Lora Polack.
        The Declaration of Independence / by Lora Polack Oberle.
                p. cm. — (Let freedom ring)
        Includes bibliographical references and index.
        Summary: Provides background information on the people and events connected with the writing of the Declaration of Independence and briefly examines the contents of the document itself.
        ISBN 0-7368-1095-1
        1. United States. Declaration of Independence—Juvenile literature. 2. United States—Politics and government—1775–1783—Juvenile literature. 3. United States—Politics and government—1783–1789—Juvenile literature. [1. United States. Declaration of Independence. 2. United States. Continental Congress. 3. United States—Politics and government—1775–1783.] I. Title. II. Series.
        E221 .O24 2002
        973.3'13—dc21   2001005003

Editorial Credits
Rebecca Aldridge, editor; Kia Bielke, cover designer, interior layout designer, and interior illustrator; Jennifer Schonborn, cover production designer; Jo Miller, photo researcher

Photo Credits
Cover: Francis G. Mayer/CORBIS (large), Joseph Sohm; Visions of America/CORBIS (small); Steve Chenn/CORBIS, 5; Hulton/Archive Pictures, 6; North Wind Picture Archives, 9, 10, 21, 29, 30, 36; The Karpeles Manuscript Library, 12; CORBIS,15; Stock Montage, Inc., 16, 35, 39; Bettmann/CORBIS, 17, 23, 26–27; National Archives, 19; National Museum of American Art, Washington DC/Art Resource, 20; Hulton Getty Archive Photos, 33; Musée de la Ville de Paris, Musée Carnavalet; Giraudon/Art Resource, NY, 41; Joseph Sohm; Visions of America/CORBIS, 43

1   2   3   4   5   6   07   06   05   04   03   02

Table of Contents

Chapter One

Whispers of Independence

On May 10, 1775, a large group of men gathered in the State House in Philadelphia. Many of these men were wealthy lawyers and merchants. Some owned large farms called plantations. Some of these men were aristocrats, or people of high social rank, who wore velvet suits, powdered wigs, and lace cuffs. Others were teachers and ministers. They were all well educated and leaders in their communities. They met in broad daylight, at a prominent, or easily seen, location in town. Everyone knew their names.

Revolutions are uprisings against a government. Today when we think of revolutions, we think of people who meet in secret. We might imagine these people in disguises or uniforms. Usually, we do not think of them as wealthy or powerful. The men who met that May day in 1775 did not necessarily look like revolutionaries, but they were. They risked their lives for something they believed in.

At the Philadelphia State House (now called Independence Hall), men from the 13 colonies challenged a powerful nation to help found their own.

These men also created one of the most important documents the world has known. This official piece of paper, the Declaration of Independence, proclaimed that America was a free nation. The Declaration contained revolutionary ideas. It said that all people have rights and all people are equal. It said when government does not work anymore, people have the right to change it.

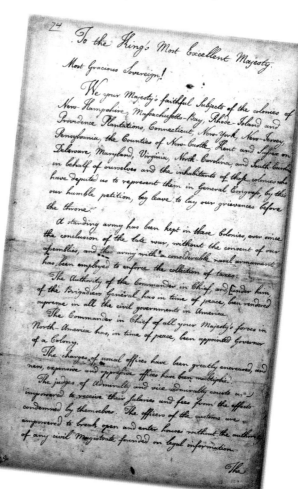

This is the first page of the petition the First Continental Congress sent to the king of Britain, hoping to settle the differences between Britain and its 13 American colonies.

The gathering of men on May 10 was the first meeting of the Second Continental Congress. These men represented each of the 13 American colonies, which belonged to Britain at that time. Colonists were upset with laws that the Parliament, Britain's government, had passed. Colonists were unhappy with the British king, George III. Colonial men gathered to discuss their complaints.

The Continental Congress had met once before in September 1774. Most of the members of the First Continental Congress wanted to find a way to get along with Britain. They did not speak openly of independence. But they did agree to boycott, or not buy, British goods. They also sent a polite petition to King George III. This signed letter asked for changes in policy.

The mood of the Second Continental Congress was different. In 1775, British soldiers had killed colonists in the Battles of Lexington and Concord in Massachusetts. These battles were the first fought in the American Revolutionary War (1775–1783). Armed men were gathering around Boston. Trouble was in the air.

Chapter Two

The Second Continental Congress

Three weeks before the Second Continental Congress met, shots were fired that started the war. On April 19, British soldiers killed eight Patriots in the small village of Lexington, Massachusetts. The soldiers were looking for hidden guns and ammunition. They also were looking for two leaders of Boston's anti-British movement, John Hancock and Samuel Adams.

Hancock and Adams escaped, but the soldiers continued on to the nearby village of Concord. There, more men were killed on both sides.

Hancock and Adams made their way to Philadelphia to join the Continental Congress. Hancock worried that other colonies would blame Massachusetts for starting the war. But people cheered as Hancock and Adams arrived, and the delegates even elected Hancock to be president of the Congress.

The Battles of Lexington (above) and Concord occurred on April 19, 1775. The Battle of Concord marked the first time Americans killed British soldiers.

Samuel Adams

Massachusetts delegate Samuel Adams was a fiery speaker. He also wrote many pamphlets, or short booklets, urging independence. Samuel was an important early leader in the Massachusetts colony.

Samuel was careless about his appearance. He often wore the same suit and it usually looked rumpled. Before he went to the First Continental Congress, his friends bought him a new suit. They did not want him to embarrass their colony.

Creating a National Army

In the mid-1700s, Britain was the mightiest nation on Earth. The British had a powerful army and navy and had recently defeated the French, another major power of the time.

The colonies had no army or navy of their own. One of the first things the Congress did was create a national army. The Continental Army would include volunteers and militias that had come to the Boston area after the Battles of Lexington and Concord.

Militias were small groups of men ready to fight in times of emergency. Each town or area had its own militia with its own leader. But there was no single leader for the 10,000 volunteers surrounding Boston. Providing that leader was the Continental Congress's next important task.

George Washington the General

On June 15, 1775, John Adams gave a long speech to the Continental Congress. Adams, a cousin of Samuel Adams, was a lawyer and a powerful speaker. He asked the Congress to name George Washington as commander in chief of the Continental Army. The delegates voted for him unanimously. Not one vote was against Washington.

Two weeks later, in July, General George Washington took charge of the Continental Army. He began to create an orderly army out of the thousands of volunteers. The British realized that the colonies were serious about the war.

Olive Branch Petition

A few members of the Continental Congress still believed that war could be stopped. So the Congress sent a petition to King George III. In this petition, the delegates suggested how he could keep the colonies loyal to Britain. They asked the king to choose the olive branch of peace over the sword of war. That is how the document became known as the Olive Branch Petition. But George III refused even to read the letter.

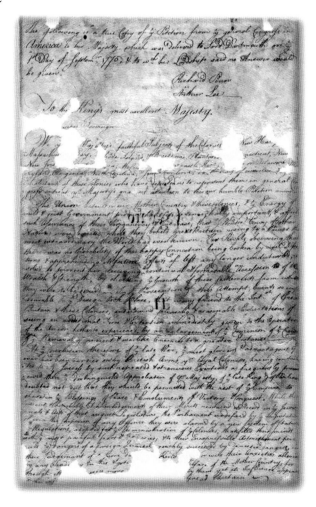

The Continental Congress sent the Olive Branch Petition to King George III, hoping to stop the war.

George Washington

Washington came to the Second Continental Congress to represent the people of the Virginia colony. He was famous as a leader in the French and Indian War (1754–1763).

When Washington arrived at the Congress on May 10, other delegates turned to notice him. Washington was wearing his military uniform again. He was ready to lead the fight that had already begun in Lexington and Concord.

It may seem odd that Congress was trying to negotiate, or work out, peace yet preparing to fight at the same time. But people had many different opinions about the fighting. It took time before it was clear that the colonists were in a revolution.

Also, the colonies did not think of themselves as parts of one large nation. They saw themselves as independent states. For example, people from New York thought of themselves as New Yorkers first and as Americans second. The colonies tried to work together in their relations with Britain. But each colony also had its own special interests. Sometimes, delegates from different colonies argued.

Chapter Three

Differences of Opinion

Americans did not all agree in their feelings about independence. Some estimates indicate that in 1776, as many as one-third of Americans were Tories. These people were still loyal to Britain. The issue of independence tore some families apart. Even delegate Benjamin Franklin's son, William, the royal governor of New Jersey, was a Tory. This fact caused Benjamin much grief.

It Is Just Common Sense

On January 9, 1776, an important booklet called *Common Sense,* written by Thomas Paine, appeared in the colonies. Paine was a British man who had come to the colonies less than two years earlier. But he was passionate about American independence.

Common Sense argued for independence. There was no going back now, it said. American freedom could never be secure under British rule. It was time for a new government free of

Thomas Paine was the author of *Common Sense*, a book that helped inspire the ideas in the Declaration of Independence.

No Profits

Thomas Paine did not
profit from *Common Sense.*
He gave the book's printer
half of the money made
from the book's sales. Paine
used the other half of the
money to buy mittens for
colonial soldiers.

COMMON SENSE;

ADDRESSED TO THE

INHABITANTS

OF

AMERICA,

On the following interesting

SUBJECTS.

I. Of the Origin and Design of Government in general, with concise Remarks on the English Constitution.

II. Of Monarchy and Hereditary Succession.

III. Thoughts on the present State of American Affairs.

IV. Of the present Ability of America, with some miscellaneous Reflections.

Man knows no Master save creating HEAVEN, Or those whom choice and common good ordain.

THOMSON.

PHILADELPHIA:

Printed, and Sold, by R. BELL, in Third-Street.

MDCCLXXVI.

kings. In this new government, power would come
from the people.

Common Sense was the best-selling book of the
time. It sold 500,000 copies during a time when
most people could not even read. Often, one person
would read this book to a group of five or six others.
Although the book sold 500,000 copies, its message
reached millions of people. Paine's booklet marked
the first time the general public began to argue
for independence.

Richard Henry Lee's Resolution

Not all the colonies agreed on independence, but
Massachusetts and Virginia were two strong
supporters of it. In May 1776, the Virginia
legislature, or government, told its delegates to
propose independence. On June 7, 1776, Richard
Henry Lee of Virginia stood up in the Congress. He
read a resolution calling for independence. His
formal statement was called the Lee Resolution.

Richard Henry Lee
read a resolution that
said in part: "These
United Colonies are,
and of right ought to be,
free and independent
States..."

Lee's Black Silk Hand

While Lee read his resolution, he moved his hand about to strengthen his words. Lee's hand was wrapped in black silk to hide the missing fingers that he had lost in a hunting accident.

When the Continental Congress voted on the Lee Resolution, only seven colonies voted for it. Delegates from other colonies wanted to get more instructions from their legislatures. The Congress decided to give these delegates three weeks.

The Committee of Five

On June 11, Congress appointed a committee to draft a declaration of independence. This group was called the Committee of Five.

Five men made up this committee. John Adams of Massachusetts and Roger Sherman of Connecticut represented the New England colonies. The Middle colonies were represented by Benjamin Franklin of Pennsylvania and Robert R. Livingston of New York, a colony especially unsure about breaking with Britain.

Thomas Jefferson of Virginia represented the Southern colonies. He was 33, one of the youngest members of the Congress. Jefferson was quiet in public and did not give long speeches. John Adams later said of Jefferson, "During the whole time I sat with him in the Congress, I never heard him utter three sentences together."

Yet Jefferson also was well known as a polished writer. So the committee asked him to write the

The Committee of Five represented the New England colonies, the Middle colonies, and the Southern colonies.

important document. They reasoned that if the author was a Southerner, it would show support for independence outside of New England. But Jefferson wanted Adams to be the author.

Years later, Adams remembered what he had told Jefferson: "Reason first—You are a Virginian, and a Virginian ought to appear at the head of this business. Reason second—I am obnoxious [annoying], suspected, and unpopular. You are very much otherwise. Reason third—You can write ten times better than I can."

In rented rooms in downtown Philadelphia (in the building shown here), Jefferson wrote and rewrote drafts of the Declaration.

Did You Know?

Thomas Jefferson wrote the Declaration of Independence at a portable desk that he had designed himself.

Jefferson Writes the Declaration

The committee met several times before Jefferson began writing. They discussed how the Declaration should be organized, and they talked about the ideas it should include. Then Jefferson started writing.

Jefferson did not have much time to write the Declaration. Congress was busy with the war, so he had to attend meetings of the Congress during the day. He belonged to other committees and had to write reports for them as well.

Jefferson worked for two-and-one-half weeks. When he was not satisfied with his work, he ripped it up. Only a small piece of one of his early drafts still exists.

Jefferson showed his finished draft to Adams and Franklin. They made just a few changes before giving it to the Congress on June 28, 1776.

Chapter Four

Making History

On July 1, the Second Continental Congress met to debate the Lee Resolution for independence. John Dickinson of Pennsylvania argued against independence, saying it was risky. He did not want the colonies to abandon the protection of Britain. He said it was "like destroying our house in winter . . . before we have got another shelter." Instead, Dickinson wanted to find a way to get along with the mother country.

As John Adams spoke for independence, a summer storm crackled in the background. Lightning flashed, and thunder rattled the windows. No record of his speech exists. But Jefferson remembered that Adams spoke "with a power of thought and expression that moved us from our seats."

John Adams was a
powerful speaker. On
July 1, 1776, when the
Congress met to debate
the Lee Resolution,
Adams argued
for independence.

A Deciding Vote

Delaware had a third delegate, Caesar Rodney, who was in favor of independence. Rodney was not in the Congress the day the unofficial vote was taken. However, he rode 80 miles (129 kilometers) through pouring rain to return to the Congress. His vote for independence broke the tie in his colony.

The unofficial vote that day was divided. Only nine colonies voted for independence. Pennsylvania and North Carolina were against it. The two delegates from Delaware were divided. New York still had not received instructions on how to vote.

The Vote That Made History

On July 2, 1776, the delegates took an official vote. Twelve of the 13 colonies voted for the Lee Resolution. New York's delegates did not vote because they still had not received instructions from their legislature. Within a few days, New York's instructions finally arrived. When the New York delegates added their vote for independence, the final total was unanimous.

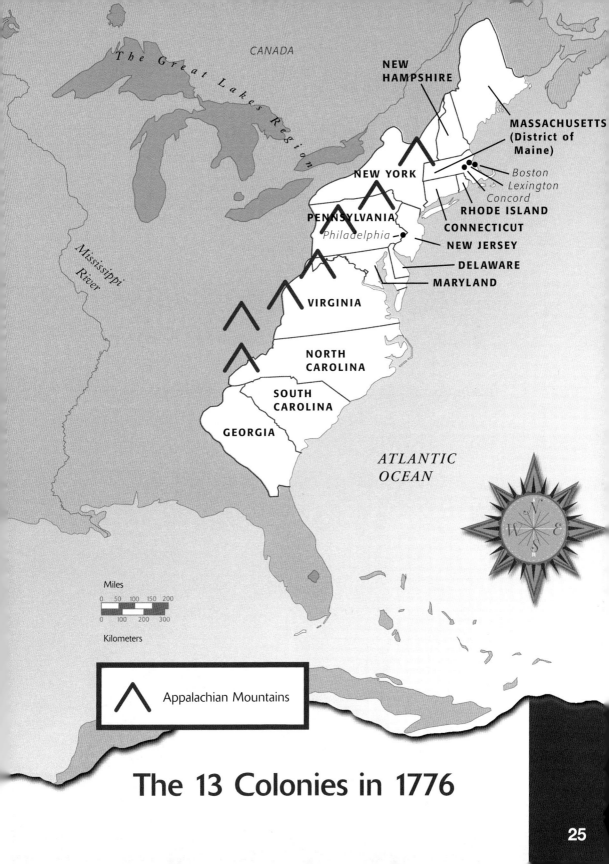

CANADA

The Great Lakes Region

NEW
HAMPSHIRE

MASSACHUSETTS
(District of
Maine)

Boston
Lexington
Concord

NEW YORK

PENNSYLVANIA

RHODE ISLAND

CONNECTICUT

Philadelphia

NEW JERSEY

DELAWARE

MARYLAND

Mississippi River

VIRGINIA

NORTH
CAROLINA

SOUTH
CAROLINA

GEORGIA

*ATLANTIC
OCEAN*

Miles

0 50 100 150 200

0   100   200   300

Kilometers

Appalachian Mountains

The 13 Colonies in 1776

Congress now had to decide how to announce the colonies' independence to the world. They turned their attention to Jefferson's draft of the Declaration of Independence.

Over the next two days, the Congress discussed the document word by word. Jefferson listened unhappily as the Congress made changes to his document. They changed words and phrases and even took out whole paragraphs. In all, Congress made about 80 changes. Finally, in the late

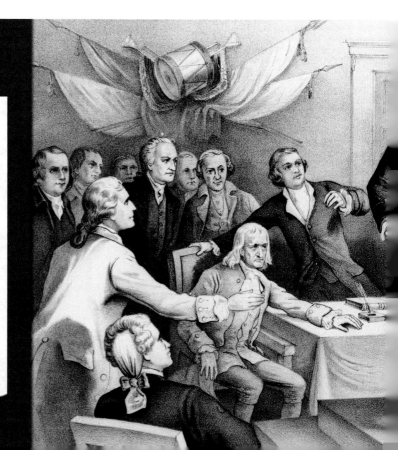

John Hancock's name is the largest on the Declaration of Independence. Hancock (shown standing) said he wanted to make his signature large enough that King George III could read it without his glasses.

Stephen Hopkins

Stephen Hopkins was a delegate from Rhode Island. He had an illness that was called "palsy" in the 1700s. It caused his hands to shake. When Hopkins signed the Declaration of Independence, he said, "My hand trembles, but my heart does not."

afternoon of July 4, the delegates were satisfied with the Declaration and were ready to sign it.

Signing Their Lives Away

John Hancock stepped forward. As president of the Congress, he was the first to sign the Declaration. He picked up the quill pen and signed his name in large, bold letters. On July 4, 1776, Hancock's signature made the Declaration legal and binding. Historians believe that the other delegates signed later, after a clean copy of the Declaration was made.

How Dangerous Was It?

None of the signers of the Declaration of Independence was ever hanged by the British. But at least five of them were captured during battles. Richard Stockton of New Jersey was dragged from bed, treated badly, and put in prison by the British. Stockton was released but then suffered from poor health. He died several years later. Francis Lewis of New York lost his home and fortune because of the war. His wife also was taken prisoner by the British.

It took courage for Hancock and the others to sign the Declaration. They knew they were putting their lives in danger by doing so. If the Americans lost the war, they could be arrested and hanged. Benjamin Rush of Pennsylvania later wrote about the "fears and sorrows and sleepless nights" they all felt.

According to one story, Hancock spoke to Franklin about all the signers sticking together after putting their names on the Declaration. Hancock told Franklin that they all had to hang together. Franklin replied, "Surely, we must all hang together, or we shall all hang separately."

The Declaration Excites the People

Church bells rang out over Philadelphia on July 4, 1776. The sound signaled that the Declaration of Independence had been accepted. The next day, a printer made copies of the Declaration. These copies were sent throughout the 13 former colonies.

Copies also were sent to Washington and other Continental Army leaders. Washington made sure that the Declaration was read aloud to his troops. The soldiers shouted happily and threw their hats in the air when they heard the document's words.

Throughout the 13 former colonies, crowds gathered to hear the Declaration of Independence read aloud.

In New York, crowds gathered to hear the Declaration read aloud. Then they pulled down a statue of George III that was in a park. Later, that statue was melted and made into bullets to fight the king's troops.

People reacted strongly to the words of the Declaration. In Boston, after the Declaration was read, crowds stormed the State House. They pulled down the King's coat of arms from the front of the building (right). People cried "God save the American states!"

The Continental Congress in War

The Continental Congress kept all their important papers, including the Declaration of Independence, together. During the war, the Congress took these papers along as they moved from place to place to keep safe.

The Congress met in Philadelphia until late 1776. They then moved to Baltimore, Maryland. In 1777, the Congress moved several times within Pennsylvania. They went from Philadelphia to Lancaster, and then to York. After 1778, the Congress came back to Philadelphia.

Soon, everyone in the 13 former colonies heard the news. Liberty had been declared, but it still had to be won. Americans had to fight a long time until the last major battle of the war was won in 1781. And it was even longer until America and Britain signed the peace treaty in 1783. The Revolutionary War officially ended with this agreement, called the Treaty of Paris. In that treaty, the British king finally recognized the 13 American states as one independent country.

Chapter Five

What the Declaration Means

The Declaration of Independence consists of three general parts. The first part is a preamble, or introduction, that presents the ideas on which the Declaration is based. It is the most famous part of the Declaration.

The preamble includes the famous words, "We hold these truths to be self-evident, that all men are created equal, that they are endowed by their Creator with certain unalienable Rights, that among these are Life, Liberty and the pursuit of Happiness."

These words of the preamble were truly revolutionary at the time they were written. They said that people's rights did not come from kings. They were natural, or God-given, rights. These rights did not have to be proved ("self-evident"). And these rights could not be taken away ("unalienable").

The Declaration of Independence includes the famous words: "We hold these truths to be self-evident, that all men are created equal…"

Jefferson's Job

"I see my job as trying to bring together and harmonize a variety of different opinions. We are putting before all of mankind words that are both simple and firm, a justification [reason] for the stand that we're being forced to take."
—Thomas Jefferson

The second part of the Declaration is the body, which lists the colonies' charges against King George III. Here, they listed the wrongs they felt he had done, such as taxing them without their approval and closing their legislatures.

In the final part of the Declaration, the colonies formally announce their independence. The signers swore their lives and all they owned to make freedom from Britain happen.

Ideas behind the Declaration

The members of the Continental Congress, including Jefferson, were familiar with a wide variety of political writers. Jefferson relied on the ideas of many of these writers when he was working on the Declaration. He said, "I did not consider it part of my charge to invent new ideas, but to place before mankind the common sense of the subject."

One idea found in the Declaration is a theory called "natural rights." Various political philosophers wrote about this theory. They included John Locke from Britain and French writer Jean Jacques Rousseau. Locke argued that people are born with natural rights. Governments, he said, should be run for the benefit of everyone, not just the rulers.

Writings by John Locke influenced the content of the Declaration of Independence.

Another idea Jefferson included in the Declaration is that of the "social contract." People come together and form governments to protect their rights. If a government fails to protect people's rights, then the people have the right to form a new government. King George III broke this social contract. He failed to protect colonists' rights.

A document Jefferson had written a few weeks earlier also influenced him. This paper was the preamble to Virginia's new, revolutionary constitution. Jefferson had a copy of an early draft among his papers.

Many people owned African slaves at the time the Declaration of Independence was written.

Celebrating July 2 Instead of July 4?

The members of the Continental Congress knew that they had done something incredibly important. John Adams believed that future Americans would celebrate their independence every year. There was only one thing he got wrong. Adams thought Americans would celebrate on July 2, the day the Lee Resolution passed. He did not know how important the Declaration itself would become.

Another document that influenced Jefferson's writing was the draft of Virginia's Declaration of Rights written by a respected plantation owner named George Mason. This document listed basic human rights the new government in Virginia should honor.

The Declaration and Slavery

When Jefferson wrote the Declaration, he included a section attacking the slave trade. He described slavery as a "cruel war against human nature." Later, he also wrote that "nothing is more certainly written in the book of fate than that these people [slaves] are to be free."

Jefferson's opinions on slavery were different from his practices. Jefferson lived in a state where it was legal to own slaves. His wealth depended on the labor of his slaves. He owned more than 200 slaves and freed only seven of them.

Other members of the Continental Congress also were clearly against slavery. John Adams gave passionate speeches against the practice. Benjamin Franklin and Benjamin Rush helped start the first antislavery society in the colonies.

But delegates from the South disagreed on the slavery issue. South Carolina and Georgia would not sign the Declaration if it contained language against slavery. Some delegates from New England supported these states because New England merchants profited from the slave trade.

The delegates argued back and forth about slavery. Finally, they realized they could not solve the issue and still remain united. All language about slavery was taken out of the Declaration of Independence. The issue of slavery would not be settled in the country until the U.S. Civil War (1861–1865).

The Declaration and Women

The Declaration contains the words "all men are created equal." It does not mention women. In the 1700s, the word *men* was often meant to include women. But women belonged to their fathers or their husbands. They were not thought to be the equals of men and did not have rights of their own.

Abigail Adams was married to John Adams. She was an intelligent and well-read woman. In her letters to John, she often asked him to "consider the ladies" in the new government. But most likely, no member of the Continental Congress ever thought seriously about women's rights.

Did You Know?

The Declaration of Independence is kept in a bulletproof glass container with a bronze frame. Helium gas fills the case to keep the Declaration from being damaged. At night, the case is lowered into a large safe of reinforced concrete and steel to keep the Declaration protected.

Over time, the values expressed in the Declaration were applied to women as well. But it took a long time before women gained their rights. It was not until 1920 that women could even vote.

The Declaration and the World

The Declaration of Independence is probably the most famous of all American documents. It defines basic American rights and liberties. These include the well-known rights to "Life, Liberty and the pursuit of Happiness." The Declaration also says that all people are equal and entitled to the same basic human rights and liberties.

The Declaration of Independence has become a standard for other countries around the world. Many people want the rights described in it.

The ideas from the American Revolution spread throughout the world. For example, in the 1790s, the French used the American Revolution as inspiration for their own revolution. One measure of the Declaration's greatness is the fact that it continues to influence people throughout the United States and the world, even today.

The French Revolution (1787–1799) was inspired by the American Revolution.

TIMELINE

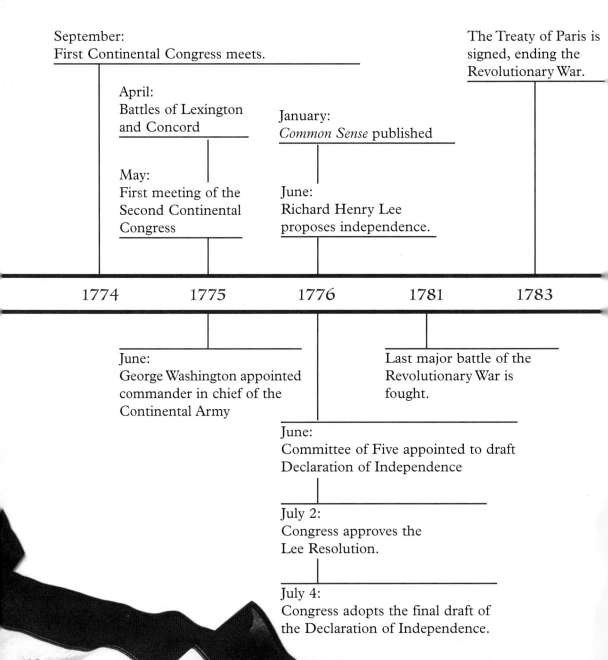

September:
First Continental Congress meets.

The Treaty of Paris is signed, ending the Revolutionary War.

April:
Battles of Lexington and Concord

January:
Common Sense published

May:
First meeting of the Second Continental Congress

June:
Richard Henry Lee proposes independence.

1774   **1775**   **1776**   **1781**   **1783**

June:
George Washington appointed commander in chief of the Continental Army

Last major battle of the Revolutionary War is fought.

June:
Committee of Five appointed to draft Declaration of Independence

July 2:
Congress approves the Lee Resolution.

July 4:
Congress adopts the final draft of the Declaration of Independence.

IN CONGRESS, JULY 4, 1776.

The unanimous Declaration of the thirteen united States of America.

Glossary

committee (kuh-MIT-ee)—a group of people chosen to discuss things and make decisions for a larger group

declaration (dek-luh-RAY-shuhn)—a public announcement

delegate (DEL-uh-guht)—a person chosen to represent other people at a meeting

document (DOK-yuh-muhnt)—an official piece of paper containing important information

independence (in-di-PEN-duhnss)—freedom from the control of others

militia (muh-LISH-uh)—a group of citizens who are trained to fight but serve only in times of emergency

Patriot (PAY-tree-uht)—a colonist loyal to America during the Revolutionary War; Patriots wanted to form a free, new nation independent of Britain.

resolution (rez-uh-LOO-shuhn)—a formal statement of a decision

revolution (rev-uh-LOO-shuhn)—a fight to replace a system of government; in the American Revolution, colonists fought against Britain and formed a new government.

Tory (TOR-ee)—a colonist loyal to King George III and Britain during the American Revolution

unanimous (yoo-NAN-uh-muhss)—agreed on by everyone

For Further Reading

Aldridge, Rebecca. *Thomas Jefferson.* Let Freedom Ring. Mankato, Minn.: Bridgestone Books, 2001.

Collier, Christopher, and James Lincoln Collier. *The American Revolution, 1763–1783.* The Drama of American History. New York: Benchmark Books, 1998.

Freedman, Russell. *Give Me Liberty!: The Story of the Declaration of Independence.* New York: Holiday House, 2000.

Hakim, Joy. *From Colonies to Country.* History of US. New York: Oxford University Press, 1999.

Todd, Anne. *The Revolutionary War.* America Goes to War. Mankato, Minn.: Capstone Books, 2001.

Places of Interest

Atwater Kent Museum
15 South Seventh Street
Philadelphia, PA 19106
Has some personal items that
belonged to Jefferson while he
was writing the Declaration
of Independence

Christ Church Burial Ground
Fifth and Arch Streets
Philadelphia, PA 19106
Many signers of the Declaration
of Independence are buried here.

Graff House
Seventh and Market Streets
Philadelphia, PA 19106
Where Jefferson wrote the
Declaration of Independence

**Independence
National Historical Park**
318 Walnut Street
Philadelphia, PA 19106
Includes many sites related to the
Revolutionary War, one of which
is Independence Hall. This is the
original Pennsylvania State House
where the Declaration of
Independence was adopted.

**Rotunda of the National
Archives Building**
700 Pennsylvania Avenue NW
Washington, DC 20408
The Declaration of Independence
is on display here.

Internet Sites

America's Story from America's Library
http://www.americaslibrary.gov/cgi-bin/page.cgi
Lets you jump back in time and explore events from many periods of
history, including the American Revolution

Colonial Hall: Biographies of the Founding Fathers
http://www.colonialhall.com/biodoi.asp
Provides information on the lives of the signers of the Declaration
of Independence

The Declaration of Independence
http://www.historychannel.com/exhibits/declaration/main.html
Lets you read the Declaration of Independence and click on parts of it
for an explanation of that part's meaning

The Declaration of Independence: A History
http://www.nara.gov/exhall/charters/declaration/dechist.html
Contains the story of the Declaration of Independence

The Declaration of Independence: A Transcription
http://www.nara.gov/exhall/charters/declaration/declaration.html
Has the complete text of the Declaration of Independence

**Founding.com: A User's Guide to the Declaration
of Independence**
http://www.founding.com/home.htm
Includes a glossary of terms found in the Declaration of Independence
and a timeline of Revolutionary events

Index